MW00438711

"Showing gratitude to the One who created you is a very powerful thing. It gives you a sense of balance and draws good into your life."

~MUFTI ISMAIL MENK~

Gratitude Journal for Muslim Women "Start With Alhamdulillah"
Quran Quotes, Daily Dua & Reflections
Cover Design by Vecteezy.com
ISBN: 9781707700516

How to use this journal?

QURAN QUOTES & REFERENCE- MORNING ROUTINE
Everyday you will be presented with a beautiful quote from the Quran
complete with the surah and verse number for quick reference.

DAILY DUA - MORNING ROUTINE
Before anything else, start your journal daily with reliance upon Allah.
Write a short dua asking Allah for help, fully aware that without His help
we are not able to do anything. Make dua about various aspects of your
life. And don't forget to make dua for the Ummah too.

GRATITUDE - MORNING ROUTINE
Reflect upon your life and write a few things that you are grateful for every
day even for the smallest thing. Perhaps the chirping of the birds or the
wonderful smell of fresh clothes. Nothing is insignificant.

SET YOUR INTENTION RIGHT - MORNING ROUTINE
The Prophet Muhammad (saw) said: "Truly, the deeds are only according
to the intentions, and to every man is that which he has intended." So, use
the third slot with the right intention. For example; "*I will try to be more
patient today because Allah loves as-Sabirin (the patient ones); Ali Imran 3:146.*"

AMAZING EXPERIENCES- EVENING ROUTINE
Ponder and write the daily event that happened which makes you happy.
By reflecting and focusing on your blessings instead of your hardships, you
will increase in gratitude and happiness, inshaa Allah.

PLANNING FOR TOMORROW - EVENING ROUTINE
This slot allows you to plan and look forward to tomorrow. Plan and write
the things you are excited about doing the next day and try to achieve them.

DAILY PRAYER TRACKER
Track your *salah* progress using this tracker and get motivated
to improve yourself every day.

MONTHLY REFLECTIONS
Every 30 days you will get two gratitude prompts about
different areas in your life. Reflect and write your thoughts on
each question as you increase the feeling of shukr towards
Allah.

The concept of gratitude in Islam

Gratitude— a simple word with a dynamic power in its meaning and application. We often forget to cultivate and practice gratitude, overlooking how life-changing it can be. An attitude of gratitude has the ability to make a harsh reality seem tolerable, giving light to a gloomy disposition and dispelling negative attitudes, thoughts, and feelings with wondrous speed.

According to Islam, one of our foremost duties is to be grateful to Allah for all of His blessings. We can describe three levels of thankfulness as such:

1. To realize and appreciate all blessings by and within the heart.
2. To say thanks with the tongue.
3. To express gratitude by doing righteous deeds.

In other words, the first level is the appreciative and gratefulness that we feel in our hearts. Then we fortify that thankfulness through our speech. And the third level is when we prove by our deeds that we are truly thankful to Allah.

Becoming More Thankful

As we open the Quran, the first chapter starts with 'Alhamdulillah' which is generally translated as "all praise is for Allah." In reality, the word Alhamdulillah signifies gratitude in our everyday lives. Hence, when someone asks how we are, Muslim often respond with, "Alhamdulillah."

Similarly, Islam teaches us to be thankful throughout the day: for waking up from sleep, after eating our meals, drinking water, etc. In this way, one's entire life revolves around gratitude to Allah.

Opportunity to Come Closer to Allah

When we are tested by a difficulty, often our first reaction is to turn to Allah for help. Whatever our spiritual state and level of faith prior to the hardship, the adversity itself has shown us how much we are in need of Allah, and the act of turning to Him through sincere prayer and du'a of yearning for His help brings us closer to Him, increases our faith, and grants us the blessings that come from increased worship. This is one of the purposes of hardship. Allah says in the Quran:

> *"And We have sundered them in the earth as [separate] nations. Some of them are righteous, and some far from that. And We have tried them with prosperity and adversity in order that they might return"*
> *(Al-A'raf 7: 168)*

The Science of Gratitude

Research done by the University of California, Berkeley, has revealed that gratitude leads to a stronger immune system, healthier blood pressure, greater joy, optimism, and sense of overall well-being, acting with more generosity and compassion, and feeling less lonely and isolated.

Participants in the study simply recorded five things they were grateful for each day. This small exercise proved to have enormous benefits. Imagine what a permanent attitude of gratitude can accomplish. And imagine when we do this purely for the sake of Allah alone, this attitude becomes an act of worship *(ibadaah)* and it can transform our lives in this world and the next.

Allahuakhbar!

How to Cultivate Gratitude?

- Let the remembrance of Allah guide you throughout the day.

- Keeping a journal is a great way to help you cultivating an attitude of gratitude towards Allah.

- Practice thanking others for the simple things they do for you; write a thank you letter (or email) to someone who has impacted your life in a positive way.

- Remember the people who are less fortunate than you, step into their shoes, empathize with their plight, and do something, even if small, to alleviate someone else's difficulty.

- When tough times set in, focus on the positives. Things could be much worse. Say Alhamdulillah upon every circumstances and reflect on your blessings.

- Remind yourself often to adopt an attitude of gratitude and smile. Remember, it's sunnah!

Date:

> "And be grateful to Allah, if it is indeed He whom you worship."
>
> SURAH AL-BAQARAH 2:172

Oh Allah, I make dua that...

Alhamdulillah, today I am truly grateful for...

Inshaa Allah, here's what would make today great...

Some amazing things that happened today, alhamdulillah...

Tomorrow I will, inshaa Allah...

Daily Prayer Tracker:

Fajr ◯   Dhuhr ◯   Asr ◯   Maghrib ◯   Isha ◯

Date:

> ## "Call upon Me, I will respond to you"
> SURAH GHAFIR 40:60

Oh Allah, I make dua that...

_____

_____

_____

_____

Alhamdulillah, today I am truly grateful for...

_____

_____

_____

_____

Inshaa Allah, here's what would make today great...

_____

_____

Some amazing things that happened today, alhamdulillah...

_____

_____

Tomorrow I will, inshaa Allah...

_____

_____

Daily Prayer Tracker:

Fajr ○   Dhuhr ○   Asr ○   Maghrib ○   Isha ○

Date:

> And Allah would not punish them
> while they seek forgiveness.
>
> SURAH AL-ANFAL 8:33

Oh Allah, I make dua that...

_____

_____

_____

_____

_____

Alhamdulillah, today I am truly grateful for...

_____

_____

_____

_____

Inshaa Allah, here's what would make today great...

_____

_____

_____

Some amazing things that happened today, alhamdulillah...

_____

_____

Tomorrow I will, inshaa Allah...

_____

_____

_____

Daily Prayer Tracker:

Fajr ◯   Dhuhr ◯   Asr ◯   Maghrib ◯   Isha ◯

Date:

So remember Me; I will remember you.

SURAH AL-BAQARAH 2:152

Oh Allah, I make dua that...

Alhamdulillah, today I am truly grateful for...

Inshaa Allah, here's what would make today great...

Some amazing things that happened today, alhamdulillah...

Tomorrow I will, inshaa Allah...

Daily Prayer Tracker:

Fajr ○   Dhuhr ○   Asr ○   Maghrib ○   Isha ○

Date:

> ## And He has made me blessed wherever I am.
> SURAH MARYAM 19:31

Oh Allah, I make dua that...

Alhamdulillah, today I am truly grateful for...

Inshaa Allah, here's what would make today great...

Some amazing things that happened today, alhamdulillah...

Tomorrow I will, inshaa Allah...

Daily Prayer Tracker:

Fajr ◯   Dhuhr ◯   Asr ◯   Maghrib ◯   Isha ◯

Date:

> He knows what is within the heavens and earth
> and knows what you conceal and what you declare.
> And Allah (swt) is Knowing of that within the breasts.
> SURAH AT-TAGHABUN 64:4

Oh Allah, I make dua that...

Alhamdulillah, today I am truly grateful for...

Inshaa Allah, here's what would make today great...

Some amazing things that happened today, alhamdulillah...

Tomorrow I will, inshaa Allah...

Daily Prayer Tracker:

Fajr ◯   Dhuhr ◯   Asr ◯   Maghrib ◯   Isha ◯

Date:

> And whoever puts all his trust in Allah,
> He will be enough for him.
>
> SURAH AT-TALAQ 65:3

Oh Allah, I make dua that...

Alhamdulillah, today I am truly grateful for...

Inshaa Allah, here's what would make today great...

Some amazing things that happened today, alhamdulillah...

Tomorrow I will, inshaa Allah...

Daily Prayer Tracker:

Fajr ◯   *Dhuhr* ◯   *Asr* ◯   *Maghrib* ◯   *Isha* ◯

Date: ....

> Indeed, those who have believed and done righteous deeds
> will have garden beneath which rivers flow.
> That is a great attainment
> SURAH AL-BURUJ 85:11

Oh Allah, I make dua that...

_____

_____

_____

_____

Alhamdulillah, today I am truly grateful for...

_____

_____

_____

Inshaa Allah, here's what would make today great...

_____

_____

Some amazing things that happened today, alhamdulillah...

_____

Tomorrow I will, inshaa Allah...

_____

_____

Daily Prayer Tracker:

Fajr ○   Dhuhr ○   Asr ○   Maghrib ○   Isha ○

Date:

> "If you are grateful, I will surely increase you [in favor]".
>
> SURAH IBRAHIM 14:7

Oh Allah, I make dua that...

_____

_____

_____

_____

Alhamdulillah, today I am truly grateful for...

_____

_____

_____

_____

Inshaa Allah, here's what would make today great...

_____

_____

Some amazing things that happened today, alhamdulillah...

_____

_____

Tomorrow I will, inshaa Allah...

_____

_____

Daily Prayer Tracker:

Fajr ○   Dhuhr ○   Asr ○   Maghrib ○   Isha ○

Date:

> ## And He found you lost and guided [you]
> SURAH AD-DUHAA 93:7

Oh Allah, I make dua that...

_____

_____

_____

Alhamdulillah, today I am truly grateful for...

_____

_____

_____

Inshaa Allah, here's what would make today great...

_____

_____

Some amazing things that happened today, alhamdulillah...

_____

_____

Tomorrow I will, inshaa Allah...

_____

_____

Daily Prayer Tracker:

Fajr ◯   Dhuhr ◯   Asr ◯   Maghrib ◯   Isha ◯

Date:

> So be patient. Indeed, the promise of Allah is truth.
>
> SURAH GHAFIR 40:55

Oh Allah, I make dua that...

Alhamdulillah, today I am truly grateful for...

Inshaa Allah, here's what would make today great...

Some amazing things that happened today, alhamdulillah...

Tomorrow I will, inshaa Allah...

Daily Prayer Tracker:

Fajr ◯   Dhuhr ◯   Asr ◯   Maghrib ◯   Isha ◯

Date:

> And fear Allah. And Allah teaches you.
> And Allah is Knowing of all things.
> SURAH AL-BAQARAH 2:282

Oh Allah, I make dua that...

Alhamdulillah, today I am truly grateful for...

Inshaa Allah, here's what would make today great...

Some amazing things that happened today, alhamdulillah...

Tomorrow I will, inshaa Allah...

Daily Prayer Tracker:

Fajr ◯   Dhuhr ◯   Asr ◯   Maghrib ◯   Isha ◯

Date: ....

> "My mercy embraces all things".
>
> SURAH AL-A'RAF 7:156

Oh Allah, I make dua that...

_____

_____

_____

_____

Alhamdulillah, today I am truly grateful for...

_____

_____

_____

_____

Inshaa Allah, here's what would make today great...

_____

_____

Some amazing things that happened today, alhamdulillah...

_____

_____

Tomorrow I will, inshaa Allah...

_____

_____

Daily Prayer Tracker:

Fajr ◯   Dhuhr ◯   Asr ◯   Maghrib ◯   Isha ◯

Date:

My success can only come from Allah

SURAH HUD 11:88

Oh Allah, I make dua that...

_____

_____

_____

_____

Alhamdulillah, today I am truly grateful for...

_____

_____

_____

_____

Inshaa Allah, here's what would make today great...

_____

_____

Some amazing things that happened today, alhamdulillah...

_____

Tomorrow I will, inshaa Allah...

_____

_____

Daily Prayer Tracker:

Fajr ○   Dhuhr ○   Asr ○   Maghrib ○   Isha ○

Date:

> And all will come to Him on the Day of Resurrection alone.
>
> SURAH MARYAM 19:95

Oh Allah, I make dua that...

_____

_____

_____

_____

Alhamdulillah, today I am truly grateful for...

_____

_____

_____

_____

Inshaa Allah, here's what would make today great...

_____

_____

Some amazing things that happened today, alhamdulillah...

_____

_____

Tomorrow I will, inshaa Allah...

_____

_____

_____

Daily Prayer Tracker:

Fajr ◯   Dhuhr ◯   Asr ◯   Maghrib ◯   Isha ◯

Date:

> But they plan, and Allah plans.
> And Allah is the best of planners.
> SURAH ALI IMRAN 3:54

Oh Allah, I make dua that...

_____

_____

_____

Alhamdulillah, today I am truly grateful for...

_____

_____

_____

Inshaa Allah, here's what would make today great...

_____

_____

Some amazing things that happened today, alhamdulillah...

_____

_____

Tomorrow I will, inshaa Allah...

_____

_____

Daily Prayer Tracker:

Fajr ○   Dhuhr ○   Asr ○   Maghrib ○   Isha ○

Date: ....

> We will test you in fear, hunger, loss of wealth, life and fruits,
> but give good tidings to the patient.
>
> SURAH TAHA 20:114

Oh Allah, I make dua that...

....

....

....

....

Alhamdulillah, today I am truly grateful for...

....

....

....

....

Inshaa Allah, here's what would make today great...

....

....

Some amazing things that happened today, alhamdulillah...

....

....

Tomorrow I will, inshaa Allah...

....

....

Daily Prayer Tracker:

Fajr ◯   Dhuhr ◯   Asr ◯   Maghrib ◯   Isha ◯

Date: _____

> Whoever does righteousness, male or female, while believing,
> We will grant them a happy life.
> SURAH AN-NAHL 16:97

Oh Allah, I make dua that...

_____

_____

_____

_____

Alhamdulillah, today I am truly grateful for...

_____

_____

_____

_____

Inshaa Allah, here's what would make today great...

_____

_____

Some amazing things that happened today, alhamdulillah...

_____

_____

Tomorrow I will, inshaa Allah...

_____

_____

Daily Prayer Tracker:

Fajr ○   Dhuhr ○   Asr ○   Maghrib ○   Isha ○

Date:

> ### And hold firmly to the rope of Allah all together
> ### and do not become divided.
>
> SURAH ALI IMRAN 3:103

Oh Allah, I make dua that...

Alhamdulillah, today I am truly grateful for...

Inshaa Allah, here's what would make today great...

Some amazing things that happened today, alhamdulillah...

Tomorrow I will, inshaa Allah...

Daily Prayer Tracker:

Fajr ○   Dhuhr ○   Asr ○   Maghrib ○   Isha ○

Date:

> ## So let not this present life deceive you.
>
> SURAH FATIR 35:5

Oh Allah, I make dua that...

_____

_____

_____

_____

Alhamdulillah, today I am truly grateful for...

_____

_____

_____

_____

Inshaa Allah, here's what would make today great...

_____

_____

Some amazing things that happened today, alhamdulillah...

_____

Tomorrow I will, inshaa Allah...

_____

_____

Daily Prayer Tracker:

Fajr ◯   Dhuhr ◯   Asr ◯   Maghrib ◯   Isha ◯

Date:

> Allah does not burden a soul beyond that it can bear.
>
> SURAH BAQARAH 2:286

Oh Allah, I make dua that...

_____
_____
_____
_____

Alhamdulillah, today I am truly grateful for...

_____
_____
_____
_____

Inshaa Allah, here's what would make today great...

_____
_____

Some amazing things that happened today, alhamdulillah...

_____
_____

Tomorrow I will, inshaa Allah...

_____
_____
_____

Daily Prayer Tracker:

Fajr ◯   Dhuhr ◯   Asr ◯   Maghrib ◯   Isha ◯

Date:

> For indeed, with hardship [will be] ease.
> Indeed, with hardship [will be] ease.
>
> SURAH ASH-SHARH 94:5-6

Oh Allah, I make dua that...

_____

_____

_____

Alhamdulillah, today I am truly grateful for...

_____

_____

_____

Inshaa Allah, here's what would make today great...

_____

_____

Some amazing things that happened today, alhamdulillah...

_____

_____

Tomorrow I will, inshaa Allah...

_____

_____

Daily Prayer Tracker:

Fajr ◯   Dhuhr ◯   Asr ◯   Maghrib ◯   Isha ◯

Date: . . . .

> So be patient. Indeed, the promise of Allah is truth.
>
> SURAH AR-RUM 30:60

Oh Allah, I make dua that...

Alhamdulillah, today I am truly grateful for...

Inshaa Allah, here's what would make today great...

Some amazing things that happened today, alhamdulillah...

Tomorrow I will, inshaa Allah...

Daily Prayer Tracker:

Fajr ◯   Dhuhr ◯   Asr ◯   Maghrib ◯   Isha ◯

Date:

> And ask for forgiveness of your Lord and repent to Him.
> Indeed, my Lord is merciful and loving.
>
> SURAH HUD 11:90

Oh Allah, I make dua that...

_____

_____

_____

_____

Alhamdulillah, today I am truly grateful for...

_____

_____

_____

_____

Inshaa Allah, here's what would make today great...

_____

_____

Some amazing things that happened today, alhamdulillah...

_____

_____

Tomorrow I will, inshaa Allah...

_____

_____

Daily Prayer Tracker:

Fajr ⚪   Dhuhr ⚪   Asr ⚪   Maghrib ⚪   Isha ⚪

Date:

> Indeed, Allah is with those who fear Him
> and those who are doers of good.
>
> SURAH AN-NAHL 16:128

Oh Allah, I make dua that...

Alhamdulillah, today I am truly grateful for...

Inshaa Allah, here's what would make today great...

Some amazing things that happened today, alhamdulillah...

Tomorrow I will, inshaa Allah...

Daily Prayer Tracker:

Fajr ◯   Dhuhr ◯   Asr ◯   Maghrib ◯   Isha ◯

Date:

> Did he not realise that Allah is watching?
> SURAH AL-ALAQ 94:14

Oh Allah, I make dua that...

Alhamdulillah, today I am truly grateful for...

Inshaa Allah, here's what would make today great...

Some amazing things that happened today, alhamdulillah...

Tomorrow I will, inshaa Allah...

Daily Prayer Tracker:

Fajr ○   Dhuhr ○   Asr ○   Maghrib ○   Isha ○

Date:

> ### And worship your Lord
> ### until there comes to you the certainty [death].
>
> SURAH AL-HIJR 15:99

Oh Allah, I make dua that...

Alhamdulillah, today I am truly grateful for...

Inshaa Allah, here's what would make today great...

Some amazing things that happened today, alhamdulillah...

Tomorrow I will, inshaa Allah...

Daily Prayer Tracker:

Fajr ○   *Dhuhr* ○   *Asr* ○   *Maghrib* ○   *Isha* ○

Date: ....

> ## And do good; indeed Allah loves the doers of good.
> SURAH AL-BAQARAH 2:195

Oh Allah, I make dua that...

_____

_____

_____

_____

Alhamdulillah, today I am truly grateful for...

_____

_____

_____

_____

Inshaa Allah, here's what would make today great...

_____

_____

Some amazing things that happened today, alhamdulillah...

_____

_____

Tomorrow I will, inshaa Allah...

_____

_____

Daily Prayer Tracker:

Fajr ◯   Dhuhr ◯   Asr ◯   Maghrib ◯   Isha ◯

Date:

> ### And Allah is the best of providers.
> SURAH AL-JUMU'AH 62:11

Oh Allah, I make dua that...

Alhamdulillah, today I am truly grateful for...

Inshaa Allah, here's what would make today great...

Some amazing things that happened today, alhamdulillah...

Tomorrow I will, inshaa Allah...

Daily Prayer Tracker:

Fajr ◯   Dhuhr ◯   Asr ◯   Maghrib ◯   Isha ◯

Date:

> Indeed, prayer prohibits immorality and wrongdoing,
> and the remembrance of Allah is greater.
>
> SURAH AL-ANKABUT 29:45

Oh Allah, I make dua that...

Alhamdulillah, today I am truly grateful for...

Inshaa Allah, here's what would make today great...

Some amazing things that happened today, alhamdulillah...

Tomorrow I will, inshaa Allah...

Daily Prayer Tracker:

Fajr ◯   Dhuhr ◯   Asr ◯   Maghrib ◯   Isha ◯

What was something you asked Allah for and it came true?

Write about someone who made a positive impact on your life.

Date:

> ### And He is with you wherever you are.
> SURAH AL-HADID 57:4

Oh Allah, I make dua that...

_____

_____

_____

_____

Alhamdulillah, today I am truly grateful for...

_____

_____

_____

_____

Inshaa Allah, here's what would make today great...

_____

_____

Some amazing things that happened today, alhamdulillah...

_____

_____

Tomorrow I will, inshaa Allah...

_____

_____

Daily Prayer Tracker:

Fajr ◯   Dhuhr ◯   Asr ◯   Maghrib ◯   Isha ◯

Date:

> Indeed, the most noble of you in the sight of Allah
> is the most righteous of you.
>
> SURAH AL-HADID 57:4

Oh Allah, I make dua that...

_____

_____

_____

_____

Alhamdulillah, today I am truly grateful for...

_____

_____

_____

_____

Inshaa Allah, here's what would make today great...

_____

_____

Some amazing things that happened today, alhamdulillah...

_____

_____

Tomorrow I will, inshaa Allah...

_____

_____

Daily Prayer Tracker:

Fajr ◯   Dhuhr ◯   Asr ◯   Maghrib ◯   Isha ◯

Date:

> The life of this world is only the enjoyment of deception.
>
> SURAH ALI IMRAN 3:185

Oh Allah, I make dua that...

_____

_____

_____

_____

Alhamdulillah, today I am truly grateful for...

_____

_____

_____

_____

Inshaa Allah, here's what would make today great...

_____

_____

_____

Some amazing things that happened today, alhamdulillah...

_____

_____

Tomorrow I will, inshaa Allah...

_____

_____

Daily Prayer Tracker:

Fajr ◯   Dhuhr ◯   Asr ◯   Maghrib ◯   Isha ◯

Date:

> ### And when I am ill, it is He who cures me.
> SURAH ASH-SHU'ARA 26:80

Oh Allah, I make dua that...

Alhamdulillah, today I am truly grateful for...

Inshaa Allah, here's what would make today great...

Some amazing things that happened today, alhamdulillah...

Tomorrow I will, inshaa Allah...

Daily Prayer Tracker:

Fajr ◯   Dhuhr ◯   Asr ◯   Maghrib ◯   Isha ◯

Date: _____

> Say, "Who is Lord of the heavens and earth?"
> Say, "Allah".
>
> SURAH AR-RAD 13:16

Oh Allah, I make dua that...

_____

_____

_____

_____

Alhamdulillah, today I am truly grateful for...

_____

_____

_____

_____

Inshaa Allah, here's what would make today great...

_____

_____

Some amazing things that happened today, alhamdulillah...

_____

_____

Tomorrow I will, inshaa Allah...

_____

_____

Daily Prayer Tracker:

Fajr ○   Dhuhr ○   Asr ○   Maghrib ○   Isha ○

Date:

> "Sufficient for us is Allah,
> and [He is] the best Disposer of affairs."
>
> SURAH ALI IMRAN 3:173

Oh Allah, I make dua that...

_____

_____

_____

_____

Alhamdulillah, today I am truly grateful for...

_____

_____

_____

_____

Inshaa Allah, here's what would make today great...

_____

_____

Some amazing things that happened today, alhamdulillah...

_____

_____

Tomorrow I will, inshaa Allah...

_____

_____

Daily Prayer Tracker:

Fajr ◯   Dhuhr ◯   Asr ◯   Maghrib ◯   Isha ◯

Date:

> And no soul perceives what it will earn tomorrow,
> and no soul perceives in what land it will die.
>
> SURAH LUQMAN 31:34

Oh Allah, I make dua that...

_____

_____

_____

_____

Alhamdulillah, today I am truly grateful for...

_____

_____

_____

Inshaa Allah, here's what would make today great...

_____

_____

Some amazing things that happened today, alhamdulillah...

_____

_____

Tomorrow I will, inshaa Allah...

_____

_____

Daily Prayer Tracker:

Fajr ○   Dhuhr ○   Asr ○   Maghrib ○   Isha ○

Date:

> And it is He who created the night and the day
> and the sun and the moon.
>
> SURAH AL-ANBIYA 21:33

Oh Allah, I make dua that...

_____

_____

_____

_____

Alhamdulillah, today I am truly grateful for...

_____

_____

_____

_____

Inshaa Allah, here's what would make today great...

_____

_____

Some amazing things that happened today, alhamdulillah...

_____

_____

Tomorrow I will, inshaa Allah...

_____

_____

Daily Prayer Tracker:

Fajr ◯   Dhuhr ◯   Asr ◯   Maghrib ◯   Isha ◯

Date:

> And We have certainly beautified the nearest heaven with stars.
>
> SURAH AL-MULK 67:5

Oh Allah, I make dua that...

_____

_____

_____

_____

Alhamdulillah, today I am truly grateful for...

_____

_____

_____

_____

Inshaa Allah, here's what would make today great...

_____

_____

Some amazing things that happened today, alhamdulillah...

_____

_____

Tomorrow I will, inshaa Allah...

_____

_____

Daily Prayer Tracker:

Fajr ◯   Dhuhr ◯   Asr ◯   Maghrib ◯   Isha ◯

Date:

> So when the Qur'an is recited, then listen to it and pay attention that you may receive mercy.
>
> SURAH AL-A'RAF 7:204

Oh Allah, I make dua that...

_____

_____

_____

_____

Alhamdulillah, today I am truly grateful for...

_____

_____

_____

_____

_____

Inshaa Allah, here's what would make today great...

_____

_____

Some amazing things that happened today, alhamdulillah...

_____

_____

Tomorrow I will, inshaa Allah...

_____

_____

_____

Daily Prayer Tracker:

Fajr ◯   Dhuhr ◯   Asr ◯   Maghrib ◯   Isha ◯

Date:

> 'If you are grateful, I will surely increase you [in favor].
>
> SURAH IBRAHIM 14:7

Oh Allah, I make dua that...

Alhamdulillah, today I am truly grateful for...

Inshaa Allah, here's what would make today great...

Some amazing things that happened today, alhamdulillah...

Tomorrow I will, inshaa Allah...

Daily Prayer Tracker:

Fajr ◯   Dhuhr ◯   Asr ◯   Maghrib ◯   Isha ◯

Date:

> So whoever does an atom's weight of good will see it.
>
> SURAH AZ-ZALZALAH 99:7

Oh Allah, I make dua that...

Alhamdulillah, today I am truly grateful for...

Inshaa Allah, here's what would make today great...

Some amazing things that happened today, alhamdulillah...

Tomorrow I will, inshaa Allah...

Daily Prayer Tracker:

Fajr ◯   Dhuhr ◯   Asr ◯   Maghrib ◯   Isha ◯

Date:

> And never say of anything, "Indeed, I will do that tomorrow,"
> Except [when adding], "If Allah wills."
>
> SURAH AL-KHAF 18:23-24

Oh Allah, I make dua that...

Alhamdulillah, today I am truly grateful for...

Inshaa Allah, here's what would make today great...

Some amazing things that happened today, alhamdulillah...

Tomorrow I will, inshaa Allah...

Daily Prayer Tracker:

Fajr ⃝   Dhuhr ⃝   Asr ⃝   Maghrib ⃝   Isha ⃝

Date:

And ever is your Lord, Seeing.

SURAH AL-FURQAN 25:20

Oh Allah, I make dua that...

Alhamdulillah, today I am truly grateful for...

Inshaa Allah, here's what would make today great...

Some amazing things that happened today, alhamdulillah...

Tomorrow I will, inshaa Allah...

Daily Prayer Tracker:

Fajr ◯   *Dhuhr* ◯   *Asr* ◯   *Maghrib* ◯   *Isha* ◯

Date:

> "Indeed, my Lord is near and responsive."
> SURAH AL-FURQAN 25:20

Oh Allah, I make dua that...

Alhamdulillah, today I am truly grateful for...

Inshaa Allah, here's what would make today great...

Some amazing things that happened today, alhamdulillah...

Tomorrow I will, inshaa Allah...

Daily Prayer Tracker:

Fajr ◯   Dhuhr ◯   Asr ◯   Maghrib ◯   Isha ◯

Date:

> And this [Qur'an] is a Book We have revealed [which is] blessed,
> so follow it and fear Allah that you may receive mercy.
>
> SURAH AL-AN'AM 6:155

Oh Allah, I make dua that...

Alhamdulillah, today I am truly grateful for...

Inshaa Allah, here's what would make today great...

Some amazing things that happened today, alhamdulillah...

Tomorrow I will, inshaa Allah...

Daily Prayer Tracker:

Fajr ◯   Dhuhr ◯   Asr ◯   Maghrib ◯   Isha ◯

Date:

> And rely upon Allah; and sufficient is Allah as Disposer of affairs.
>
> SURAH AL-AHZAB 33:3

Oh Allah, I make dua that...

_____

_____

_____

Alhamdulillah, today I am truly grateful for...

_____

_____

_____

Inshaa Allah, here's what would make today great...

_____

_____

Some amazing things that happened today, alhamdulillah...

_____

_____

Tomorrow I will, inshaa Allah...

_____

_____

Daily Prayer Tracker:

Fajr ◯   Dhuhr ◯   Asr ◯   Maghrib ◯   Isha ◯

Date:

> If Allah helps you, none can overcome you;
> and if He forsakes you, who is there that can help you?
>
> SURAH ALI IMRAN 3:160

Oh Allah, I make dua that...

Alhamdulillah, today I am truly grateful for...

Inshaa Allah, here's what would make today great...

Some amazing things that happened today, alhamdulillah...

Tomorrow I will, inshaa Allah...

Daily Prayer Tracker:

Fajr ◯   Dhuhr ◯   Asr ◯   Maghrib ◯   Isha ◯

Date:

> And whoever is guided is only guided for [the benefit of] himself.
>
> SURAH AN-NAML 27:92

Oh Allah, I make dua that...

Alhamdulillah, today I am truly grateful for...

Inshaa Allah, here's what would make today great...

Some amazing things that happened today, alhamdulillah...

Tomorrow I will, inshaa Allah...

Daily Prayer Tracker:

Fajr ○   Dhuhr ○   Asr ○   Maghrib ○   Isha ○

Date: ....

> ## And seek help through patience and prayer.
> SURAH AL-BAQARAH 2:45

Oh Allah, I make dua that...

_____

_____

_____

_____

Alhamdulillah, today I am truly grateful for...

_____

_____

_____

_____

Inshaa Allah, here's what would make today great...

_____

_____

Some amazing things that happened today, alhamdulillah...

_____

_____

Tomorrow I will, inshaa Allah...

_____

_____

Daily Prayer Tracker:

Fajr ◯   Dhuhr ◯   Asr ◯   Maghrib ◯   Isha ◯

Date:

> So by your Lord, We will surely question them all,
> about what they used to do.
>
> SURAH AL-HIJR 15:92-93

Oh Allah, I make dua that...

_____

_____

_____

_____

_____

Alhamdulillah, today I am truly grateful for...

_____

_____

_____

_____

Inshaa Allah, here's what would make today great...

_____

_____

Some amazing things that happened today, alhamdulillah...

_____

_____

Tomorrow I will, inshaa Allah...

_____

_____

Daily Prayer Tracker:

Fajr ◯   Dhuhr ◯   Asr ◯   Maghrib ◯   Isha ◯

Date: ....

> And do not pursue that of which you have no knowledge.
> And do not walk upon the earth exultantly.
>
> SURAH AL-ISRA 17:36-37

Oh Allah, I make dua that...

_____
_____
_____
_____

Alhamdulillah, today I am truly grateful for...

_____
_____
_____
_____

Inshaa Allah, here's what would make today great...

_____
_____

Some amazing things that happened today, alhamdulillah...

_____
_____

Tomorrow I will, inshaa Allah...

_____
_____

Daily Prayer Tracker:

Fajr ◯   Dhuhr ◯   Asr ◯   Maghrib ◯   Isha ◯

Date:

> Then when you have taken a decision, put your trust in Allah.
>
> SURAH ALI IMRAN 3:159

Oh Allah, I make dua that...

Alhamdulillah, today I am truly grateful for...

Inshaa Allah, here's what would make today great...

Some amazing things that happened today, alhamdulillah...

Tomorrow I will, inshaa Allah...

Daily Prayer Tracker:

Fajr ◯   Dhuhr ◯   Asr ◯   Maghrib ◯   Isha ◯

Date:

> And He gave you from all you asked of Him.
>
> SURAH IBRAHIM 14:34

Oh Allah, I make dua that...

_____

_____

_____

_____

Alhamdulillah, today I am truly grateful for...

_____

_____

_____

_____

Inshaa Allah, here's what would make today great...

_____

_____

Some amazing things that happened today, alhamdulillah...

_____

_____

Tomorrow I will, inshaa Allah...

_____

_____

Daily Prayer Tracker:

Fajr ◯   Dhuhr ◯   Asr ◯   Maghrib ◯   Isha ◯

Date:

> He gives wisdom to whom He wills. And whoever
> has been given wisdom has certainly been given much good.
>
> SURAH BAQARAH 2:269

Oh Allah, I make dua that...

Alhamdulillah, today I am truly grateful for...

Inshaa Allah, here's what would make today great...

Some amazing things that happened today, alhamdulillah...

Tomorrow I will, inshaa Allah...

Daily Prayer Tracker:

Fajr ◯   Dhuhr ◯   Asr ◯   Maghrib ◯   Isha ◯

Date: _____

> Do whatever you wish. He is watchful of whatever you do.
>
> SURAH FUSSILAT 41:40

Oh Allah, I make dua that...

_____

_____

_____

_____

Alhamdulillah, today I am truly grateful for...

_____

_____

_____

_____

Inshaa Allah, here's what would make today great...

_____

_____

Some amazing things that happened today, alhamdulillah...

_____

_____

Tomorrow I will, inshaa Allah...

_____

_____

Daily Prayer Tracker:

Fajr ○   Dhuhr ○   Asr ○   Maghrib ○   Isha ○

Date:

> ## Indeed, He does not like the arrogant.
> SURAH AN-NAHL 16:23

Oh Allah, I make dua that...

_____

_____

_____

_____

Alhamdulillah, today I am truly grateful for...

_____

_____

_____

_____

Inshaa Allah, here's what would make today great...

_____

_____

Some amazing things that happened today, alhamdulillah...

_____

_____

Tomorrow I will, inshaa Allah...

_____

_____

Daily Prayer Tracker:

Fajr ○   Dhuhr ○   Asr ○   Maghrib ○   Isha ○

Date:

> ## Indeed, Allah forgives all sins.
>
> SURAH AZ-ZUMAR 39:53

Oh Allah, I make dua that...

_____

_____

_____

_____

Alhamdulillah, today I am truly grateful for...

_____

_____

_____

_____

Inshaa Allah, here's what would make today great...

_____

_____

Some amazing things that happened today, alhamdulillah...

_____

_____

Tomorrow I will, inshaa Allah...

_____

_____

Daily Prayer Tracker:

Fajr ◯   Dhuhr ◯   Asr ◯   Maghrib ◯   Isha ◯

Date:

> Be just; that is nearer to righteousness. And fear Allah.
>
> SURAH AL-MA'IDAH 5:8

Oh Allah, I make dua that...

_____

_____

_____

Alhamdulillah, today I am truly grateful for...

_____

_____

_____

Inshaa Allah, here's what would make today great...

_____

_____

Some amazing things that happened today, alhamdulillah...

_____

_____

Tomorrow I will, inshaa Allah...

_____

_____

Daily Prayer Tracker:

Fajr ○   Dhuhr ○   Asr ○   Maghrib ○   Isha ○

Date:

> So be patient; indeed, the [best] outcome is for the righteous.
>
> SURAH HUD 11:49

Oh Allah, I make dua that...

_____

_____

_____

_____

Alhamdulillah, today I am truly grateful for...

_____

_____

_____

_____

Inshaa Allah, here's what would make today great...

_____

_____

Some amazing things that happened today, alhamdulillah...

_____

_____

Tomorrow I will, inshaa Allah...

_____

_____

Daily Prayer Tracker:

Fajr ◯   Dhuhr ◯   Asr ◯   Maghrib ◯   Isha ◯

What are you thankful for about being a Muslim?

What is something that was hard to do but you did it anyway?

Date:

> And Allah wants to lighten for you [your difficulties];
> and mankind was created weak.
>
> SURAH AN-NISA 4:28

Oh Allah, I make dua that...

_____

_____

_____

_____

Alhamdulillah, today I am truly grateful for...

_____

_____

_____

_____

Inshaa Allah, here's what would make today great...

_____

_____

Some amazing things that happened today, alhamdulillah...

_____

_____

Tomorrow I will, inshaa Allah...

_____

_____

Daily Prayer Tracker:

Fajr ○   Dhuhr ○   Asr ○   Maghrib ○   Isha ○

Date:

> And there is no creature on earth but that upon Allah is its
> provision.
>
> SURAH HUD 11:6

Oh Allah, I make dua that...

_____

_____

_____

Alhamdulillah, today I am truly grateful for...

_____

_____

_____

_____

Inshaa Allah, here's what would make today great...

_____

_____

Some amazing things that happened today, alhamdulillah...

_____

_____

Tomorrow I will, inshaa Allah...

_____

_____

Daily Prayer Tracker:

Fajr ◯   Dhuhr ◯   Asr ◯   Maghrib ◯   Isha ◯

Date:

"Peace," a word from a Merciful Lord.

SURAH YA-SIN 36:58

Oh Allah, I make dua that...

Alhamdulillah, today I am truly grateful for...

Inshaa Allah, here's what would make today great...

Some amazing things that happened today, alhamdulillah...

Tomorrow I will, inshaa Allah...

Daily Prayer Tracker:

Fajr ◯   Dhuhr ◯   Asr ◯   Maghrib ◯   Isha ◯

Date:

> ## Every soul will taste death.
> SURAH ALI IMRAN 3:185

Oh Allah, I make dua that...

_____

_____

_____

Alhamdulillah, today I am truly grateful for...

_____

_____

_____

Inshaa Allah, here's what would make today great...

_____

_____

Some amazing things that happened today, alhamdulillah...

_____

_____

Tomorrow I will, inshaa Allah...

_____

_____

Daily Prayer Tracker:

Fajr ◯   Dhuhr ◯   Asr ◯   Maghrib ◯   Isha ◯

Date:

> To Allah is your return, and He is Able to do all things.
>
> SURAH HUD 11:4

Oh Allah, I make dua that...

_____
_____
_____
_____

Alhamdulillah, today I am truly grateful for...

_____
_____
_____
_____

Inshaa Allah, here's what would make today great...

_____
_____

Some amazing things that happened today, alhamdulillah...

_____
_____

Tomorrow I will, inshaa Allah...

_____
_____

Daily Prayer Tracker:

Fajr ◯   Dhuhr ◯   Asr ◯   Maghrib ◯   Isha ◯

Date:

> Allah will not change the condition of a people
> until they change what is in their hearts.
> SURAH AR-RA'D 13:11

Oh Allah, I make dua that...

Alhamdulillah, today I am truly grateful for...

Inshaa Allah, here's what would make today great...

Some amazing things that happened today, alhamdulillah...

Tomorrow I will, inshaa Allah...

Daily Prayer Tracker:

Fajr ○   Dhuhr ○   Asr ○   Maghrib ○   Isha ○

Date:

> ## So endure patiently, with beautiful patience.
> SURAH AL-MA'ARIJ 70:5

Oh Allah, I make dua that...

Alhamdulillah, today I am truly grateful for...

Inshaa Allah, here's what would make today great...

Some amazing things that happened today, alhamdulillah...

Tomorrow I will, inshaa Allah...

Daily Prayer Tracker:

Fajr ◯   Dhuhr ◯   Asr ◯   Maghrib ◯   Isha ◯

Date:

> Whoever receives guidance, receives it for his own benefit.
> Whoever goes astray, does so to his own loss.
>
> SURAH AL-ISRA 17:15

Oh Allah, I make dua that...

Alhamdulillah, today I am truly grateful for...

Inshaa Allah, here's what would make today great...

Some amazing things that happened today, alhamdulillah...

Tomorrow I will, inshaa Allah...

Daily Prayer Tracker:

Fajr ○   Dhuhr ○   Asr ○   Maghrib ○   Isha ○

Date: ....

> "Do not be afraid; I am with you all the time,
> listening and seeing."
>
> SURAH TA-HA 20:46

Oh Allah, I make dua that...

_____

_____

_____

_____

Alhamdulillah, today I am truly grateful for...

_____

_____

_____

_____

Inshaa Allah, here's what would make today great...

_____

_____

Some amazing things that happened today, alhamdulillah...

_____

_____

Tomorrow I will, inshaa Allah...

_____

_____

Daily Prayer Tracker:

Fajr ○   Dhuhr ○   Asr ○   Maghrib ○   Isha ○

Date:

Do not be sad, indeed Allah is with us.

SURAH AT-TAWBAH 9:40

Oh Allah, I make dua that...

Alhamdulillah, today I am truly grateful for...

Inshaa Allah, here's what would make today great...

Some amazing things that happened today, alhamdulillah...

Tomorrow I will, inshaa Allah...

Daily Prayer Tracker:

Fajr ◯   Dhuhr ◯   Asr ◯   Maghrib ◯   Isha ◯

Date:

> And mankind have not been given of knowledge except a little.
>
> SURAH AL-ISRA 17:85

Oh Allah, I make dua that...

Alhamdulillah, today I am truly grateful for...

Inshaa Allah, here's what would make today great...

Some amazing things that happened today, alhamdulillah...

Tomorrow I will, inshaa Allah...

Daily Prayer Tracker:

Fajr ○   Dhuhr ○   Asr ○   Maghrib ○   Isha ○

Date:

> Seek help through patience and prayer.
> Indeed, Allah is with the patient.
> SURAH AL-BAQARAH 2:153

Oh Allah, I make dua that...

_____
_____
_____
_____

Alhamdulillah, today I am truly grateful for...

_____
_____
_____
_____

Inshaa Allah, here's what would make today great...

_____
_____

Some amazing things that happened today, alhamdulillah...

_____
_____

Tomorrow I will, inshaa Allah...

_____
_____

Daily Prayer Tracker:

Fajr ◯   Dhuhr ◯   Asr ◯   Maghrib ◯   Isha ◯

Date:

> If Allah knows any good in your hearts, He will give you
> something better than what has been taken from you.
> SURAH AL-ANFAL 8:70

Oh Allah, I make dua that...

Alhamdulillah, today I am truly grateful for...

Inshaa Allah, here's what would make today great...

Some amazing things that happened today, alhamdulillah...

Tomorrow I will, inshaa Allah...

Daily Prayer Tracker:

Fajr ○   Dhuhr ○   Asr ○   Maghrib ○   Isha ○

Date:

> Do not claim yourselves to be pure. He is Most Knowing of who is pious.
>
> SURAH AN-NAJM 53:32

Oh Allah, I make dua that...

_____

_____

_____

Alhamdulillah, today I am truly grateful for...

_____

_____

_____

Inshaa Allah, here's what would make today great...

_____

_____

Some amazing things that happened today, alhamdulillah...

_____

Tomorrow I will, inshaa Allah...

_____

_____

Daily Prayer Tracker:

Fajr ◯   Dhuhr ◯   Asr ◯   Maghrib ◯   Isha ◯

Date:

> [The time of] people's judgment has drawn near,
> yet they are heedlessly turning away.
>
> SURAH AN-NAJM 53:32

Oh Allah, I make dua that...

Alhamdulillah, today I am truly grateful for...

Inshaa Allah, here's what would make today great...

Some amazing things that happened today, alhamdulillah...

Tomorrow I will, inshaa Allah...

Daily Prayer Tracker:

Fajr ◯   Dhuhr ◯   Asr ◯   Maghrib ◯   Isha ◯

Date:

Oh Allah, I make dua that...

Alhamdulillah, today I am truly grateful for...

Inshaa Allah, here's what would make today great...

Some amazing things that happened today, alhamdulillah...

Tomorrow I will, inshaa Allah...

Daily Prayer Tracker:

Fajr ◯   Dhuhr ◯   Asr ◯   Maghrib ◯   Isha ◯

Date:

> Help each other in righteousness and piety,
> but do not help one another in sin and transgression.
> SURAH AT-TARIQ 86:13-14

Oh Allah, I make dua that...

Alhamdulillah, today I am truly grateful for...

Inshaa Allah, here's what would make today great...

Some amazing things that happened today, alhamdulillah...

Tomorrow I will, inshaa Allah...

Daily Prayer Tracker:

Fajr ◯   Dhuhr ◯   Asr ◯   Maghrib ◯   Isha ◯

Date:

Oh Allah, I make dua that...

Alhamdulillah, today I am truly grateful for...

Inshaa Allah, here's what would make today great...

Some amazing things that happened today, alhamdulillah...

Tomorrow I will, inshaa Allah...

Daily Prayer Tracker:

Fajr ◯   Dhuhr ◯   Asr ◯   Maghrib ◯   Isha ◯

Date:

> And the next life is certainly far better for you than this one.
> SURAH AD-DUHAA 93:4

Oh Allah, I make dua that...

Alhamdulillah, today I am truly grateful for...

Inshaa Allah, here's what would make today great...

Some amazing things that happened today, alhamdulillah...

Tomorrow I will, inshaa Allah...

Daily Prayer Tracker:

Fajr ◯   Dhuhr ◯   Asr ◯   Maghrib ◯   Isha ◯

Date:

Surely Allah does not break His promise.

SURAH ALI IMRAN 3:9

Oh Allah, I make dua that...

Alhamdulillah, today I am truly grateful for...

Inshaa Allah, here's what would make today great...

Some amazing things that happened today, alhamdulillah...

Tomorrow I will, inshaa Allah...

Daily Prayer Tracker:

Fajr ◯   Dhuhr ◯   Asr ◯   Maghrib ◯   Isha ◯

Date:

> "I will call upon my Rabb and I am sure my prayers to my Rabb
> will not be ignored."
>
> SURAH MARYAM 19:48

Oh Allah, I make dua that...

Alhamdulillah, today I am truly grateful for...

Inshaa Allah, here's what would make today great...

Some amazing things that happened today, alhamdulillah...

Tomorrow I will, inshaa Allah...

Daily Prayer Tracker:

Fajr ○   Dhuhr ○   Asr ○   Maghrib ○   Isha ○

Date:

> And be good [to others] as Allah has been good to you.
>
> SURAH AL-QASAS 28:77

Oh Allah, I make dua that...

Alhamdulillah, today I am truly grateful for...

Inshaa Allah, here's what would make today great...

Some amazing things that happened today, alhamdulillah...

Tomorrow I will, inshaa Allah...

Daily Prayer Tracker:

Fajr ◯   Dhuhr ◯   Asr ◯   Maghrib ◯   Isha ◯

Date:

> And honor your parents. Never say to them [even] 'ugh,'
> nor yell at them. Rather, address them respectfully.
> SURAH AL-ISRA 17:23

Oh Allah, I make dua that...

Alhamdulillah, today I am truly grateful for...

Inshaa Allah, here's what would make today great...

Some amazing things that happened today, alhamdulillah...

Tomorrow I will, inshaa Allah...

Daily Prayer Tracker:

Fajr ○   Dhuhr ○   Asr ○   Maghrib ○   Isha ○

Date:

Allah is the Light of the heavens and the earth.

SURAH AN-NUR 24:35

Oh Allah, I make dua that...

Alhamdulillah, today I am truly grateful for...

Inshaa Allah, here's what would make today great...

Some amazing things that happened today, alhamdulillah...

Tomorrow I will, inshaa Allah...

Daily Prayer Tracker:

Fajr ◯   Dhuhr ◯   Asr ◯   Maghrib ◯   Isha ◯

> Indeed, We have created everything, perfectly preordained.
> SURAH AL-QAMAR 54:49

Oh Allah, I make dua that...

_____

_____

_____

_____

Alhamdulillah, today I am truly grateful for...

_____

_____

_____

_____

Inshaa Allah, here's what would make today great...

_____

_____

_____

Some amazing things that happened today, alhamdulillah...

_____

_____

Tomorrow I will, inshaa Allah...

_____

_____

_____

Daily Prayer Tracker:

Fajr ◯   Dhuhr ◯   Asr ◯   Maghrib ◯   Isha ◯

Date:

> Allah is the ally of those who believe. He brings them out from darkness into the light.
> SURAH AL-BAQARAH 2:257

Oh Allah, I make dua that...

_____

_____

_____

_____

Alhamdulillah, today I am truly grateful for...

_____

_____

_____

_____

Inshaa Allah, here's what would make today great...

_____

_____

Some amazing things that happened today, alhamdulillah...

_____

_____

Tomorrow I will, inshaa Allah...

_____

_____

Daily Prayer Tracker:

Fajr ◯   Dhuhr ◯   Asr ◯   Maghrib ◯   Isha ◯

Date:

> Allah loves those who persevere.
> SURAH ALI IMRAN 3:146

Oh Allah, I make dua that...

_____
_____
_____
_____

Alhamdulillah, today I am truly grateful for...

_____
_____
_____
_____

Inshaa Allah, here's what would make today great...

_____
_____

Some amazing things that happened today, alhamdulillah...

_____
_____

Tomorrow I will, inshaa Allah...

_____
_____
_____

Daily Prayer Tracker:

Fajr ◯   Dhuhr ◯   Asr ◯   Maghrib ◯   Isha ◯

Date:

> Fear Allah, surely Allah is aware of all your actions.
>
> SURAH AL-HASHR 59:18

Oh Allah, I make dua that...

_____

_____

_____

Alhamdulillah, today I am truly grateful for...

_____

_____

_____

Inshaa Allah, here's what would make today great...

_____

_____

Some amazing things that happened today, alhamdulillah...

_____

_____

Tomorrow I will, inshaa Allah...

_____

_____

Daily Prayer Tracker:

Fajr ◯   Dhuhr ◯   Asr ◯   Maghrib ◯   Isha ◯

Date:

> Do not flaunt yourselves as was the flaunting of finery in the
> earlier times of ignorance
>
> SURAH AL-AHZAB 33:33

Oh Allah, I make dua that...

_____

_____

_____

_____

Alhamdulillah, today I am truly grateful for...

_____

_____

_____

_____

Inshaa Allah, here's what would make today great...

_____

_____

Some amazing things that happened today, alhamdulillah...

_____

_____

Tomorrow I will, inshaa Allah...

_____

_____

Daily Prayer Tracker:

Fajr ◯   Dhuhr ◯   Asr ◯   Maghrib ◯   Isha ◯

Date:

> But those who believe, are stronger in love for Allah.
>
> SURAH AL-BAQARAH 2:165

Oh Allah, I make dua that...

_____

_____

_____

_____

Alhamdulillah, today I am truly grateful for...

_____

_____

_____

_____

Inshaa Allah, here's what would make today great...

_____

_____

Some amazing things that happened today, alhamdulillah...

_____

_____

Tomorrow I will, inshaa Allah...

_____

_____

Daily Prayer Tracker:

Fajr ◯   Dhuhr ◯   Asr ◯   Maghrib ◯   Isha ◯

Write about someplace you've been that you're grateful for.

What painful experience has helped you grow?

Notes:

Notes:

Made in the USA
Las Vegas, NV
12 March 2022